What's happening to me?

Alex Frith
Illustrated by Adam Larkum

Designed by Neil Francis
Edited by Susan Meredith

Consultants: Dr. Jeremy Kirk,
Revd Professor Michael J. Reiss & Katie Kirk, RSCN, RHV

Contents

Growing up

You've been growing up little by little ever since you were born, but there's a time when you'll start to alter a lot. That's when you begin to change from a child into an adult, and it's what this book is all about.

You might have noticed some changes happening to you already, or maybe there haven't been any yet. They don't happen to everyone at the same age and you can't tell in advance when they'll happen to you. But read the next few pages and you'll get some idea of what to expect, and when.

Perhaps you're looking forward to growing up, or maybe you have doubts. Don't worry – the changes take place gradually, so you'll have plenty of time to get used to them.

This new phase of life is called puberty, and it's mostly to do with sex. Sex is the way people make babies. Some people are embarrassed to talk about it, especially with children. Don't worry – this book explains sex, too.

> Um... Ask me again when you're older.

> Dad, where do babies come from?

Growing up is easier if you take good care of yourself. Towards the end of the book, you'll find tips for doing just that, including eating well, getting exercise and coping with other people.

When will it happen?

Most boys notice the first signs of growing up when they're about 12 or 13. Some boys might notice them before they are 10, and others not until they are 16. Most of the changes finish by the time a boy turns 18, but some of them can take a bit longer.

Same age, different stage

It's perfectly normal to develop at a different time from your friends. It doesn't matter who is the oldest in your class, or the tallest, or who eats the most. People start puberty when their bodies are ready, and not before. It can be a bit embarrassing if you are the first in your class to start, and frustrating if you are the last. But it does happen to everyone eventually, and everyone gets to the same stage in the end.

Your body needs an energy store before it can cope with all the growing that happens. So don't worry if you put on some weight – it's quite normal at this time of life.

What next?

Just so you know what to expect, here's a list of growing-up changes. Most of them overlap each other, and they don't necessarily happen to everyone in this order.

Your body will grow taller and wider.

Your face will get longer.

You will grow hair in new places.

Your voice will get deeper.

You will start to sweat more and may smell.

Your penis and testicles will get bigger.

You will start making sperm.

You might get spots, and greasy hair and skin.

Some of these changes are very obvious and you can't hide them even if you want to. You might only notice others if someone points them out to you.

Dude, you smell bad. Buy some deodorant!

Becoming a man

These changes might make you look like an adult, but it takes a few more years before you'll be treated like one. In many countries and states you have to wait until your 18th birthday before you're considered to be an adult, even though you might feel like one before that. Having an adult body doesn't mean you have an adult mind!

Taller and stronger

"Haven't you grown!" You've probably heard this from your aunts or uncles, and you're going to hear it a lot more when you start changing. Getting taller is one of the most obvious things that will happen to you, and it can start quite suddenly.

That's another load of clothes too small. More shopping...

A growth spurt

Boys usually grow fastest around the time they're 14, but you may grow tall when you're quite a bit younger or older than this. In just one year, a boy can add 7-12cm (3-5in) to his height. This is called a growth spurt, although some boys grow more gradually. If you start your growth spurt young, the chances are you'll stop growing young too. If you start your growth spurt later, you might catch up with the early growers and even overtake them.

You don't just get taller – your bones, muscles and internal organs all get bigger when you grow. In particular, your shoulders will broaden out, which makes you stronger and balances out your extra height. All this growing can keep happening into your early 20s.

Looking funny

Many boys' hands and feet get bigger first, then their arms and legs, then their body. Because of this, you might think you look really gangly. Your nose and jaw change shape too, which can make you imagine that your face looks weird before it evens out. But other people won't notice these changes as much as you do.

Getting muscley

How strong and how tall you get both depend a lot on what you inherit from your parents. This means that some boys are naturally stronger than others, just because their bones and muscles grow more. It's not just about inheritance, though. Everyone needs to eat healthily and to get some exercise every day.

Breasts

Wait a minute – isn't that something that happens to girls? Well, yes. But nearly half of all boys find that they develop slight breasts, which can be quite tender. This doesn't mean you're turning into a girl! The swelling should disappear as you become more grown up.

Voice of doom

In the middle of your throat you'll find your larynx. It's also called your voice box, because it's the part of you that you use to talk. Over the next few years, your larynx will get bigger and change shape slightly, giving you the deep, booming voice of an adult.

You make sounds by breathing out air through the vocal cords in your larynx.

Your vocal cords and larynx will both get larger – so you will make a deeper sound.

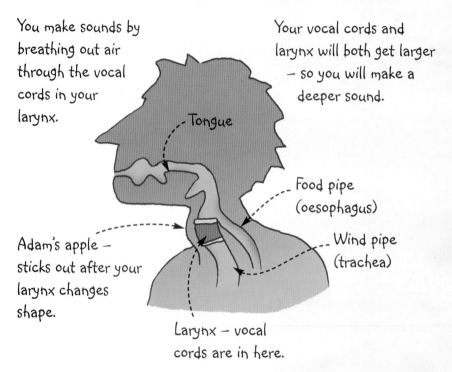

Tongue

Food pipe (oesophagus)

Adam's apple – sticks out after your larynx changes shape.

Wind pipe (trachea)

Larynx – vocal cords are in here.

Breaking your voice

When someone tells you that your voice has broken, all they mean is that it's got deeper. There's no moment when your voice actually breaks; in fact, nothing breaks at all – you just start to sound like an adult. You can already make your voice sound higher or lower if you try. Once it has broken, though, there's a limit to how high you can go, and your normal speaking voice will stay quite low.

Speaking and squeaking

It can take a while for your voice to break fully. Annoyingly, it also takes time to get used to the bigger muscles in your larynx. Sometimes these get out of control while you're talking. When this happens, one or two words will come out squeaky in the middle of a sentence, often when you're excited. It's a bit embarrassing, it's usually funny, and it happens to just about everyone.

Whose voice?

By the time your voice finishes breaking, you will sound quite different. You won't notice it yourself, but anyone who hasn't heard you for a year or two might not recognize your voice any more. Don't be surprised if people on the phone mistake you for your dad – especially strangers.

Like all the other growing-up changes, your voice might break a lot earlier or later than your friends'. It might take a while, but everyone sounds a little deeper in the end – even girls.

Getting hairy

Seeing hair grow on your body is an odd experience. You'll notice your friends start to get hairy, too, but you won't all grow hair at the same time, or even in all the same places. But here's what you might expect:

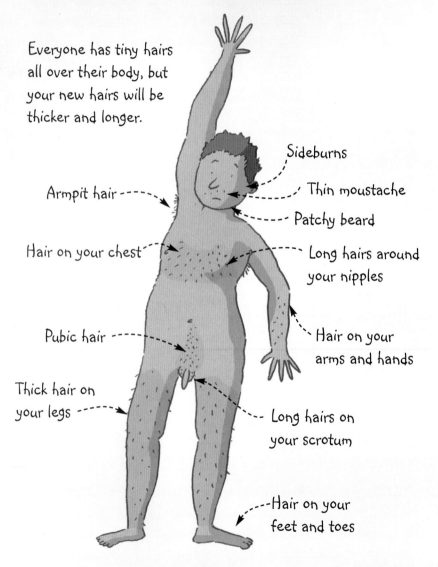

Everyone has tiny hairs all over their body, but your new hairs will be thicker and longer.

Armpit hair

Hair on your chest

Pubic hair

Thick hair on your legs

Sideburns

Thin moustache

Patchy beard

Long hairs around your nipples

Hair on your arms and hands

Long hairs on your scrotum

Hair on your feet and toes

If you shave off any body hair, you'll find that it grows back in a few days – and it will be itchy at first.

What, even there?

Everyone grows armpit and pubic hair soon after puberty starts, but face, chest and other body hair usually grows later, and some boys hardly grow any at all. Your pubic hair is usually the first to grow. To start with, it's quite thin and only grows in a small patch. After about a year it gets thicker, curlier, and spreads outwards a little bit.

Hair can grow just about anywhere on your body, even in places you can't see:
on your shoulders,
on your back,
around your bum,
in your bellybutton,
and in your nose and ears.

Hair worries

With all this hair you might think you'll turn into a werewolf before long. In fact, only the hair on your head can grow very long. The rest of it stays short. You might also worry that your friends are showing off how much hair they've got, when you don't have any at all. There's nothing wrong with having lots of hair, or very little; different people find men attractive either way.

Beard and body hair can be a different shade from the hair on your head. Fair-haired boys often grow dark pubic hair, for example. And, if your body hair is very light, it can be hard to see even when it's fully grown.

Shaving

When you start growing hair on your face, you might want to shave it off, especially because it will look patchy and messy for a few years. Not everybody shaves, though.

How often and what with?

Some people get a full beard very quickly, but most boys find that the hair grows slowly to start with. Usually, the first bit to grow is a wispy moustache, and you might need to shave this more often than the rest of your beard. After shaving, your hair grows back as stubble. Most men shave when they can feel stubble against their hand – typically once a day. Teenagers might only need to shave once a week at first. If you can't feel stubble, it's best not to shave, as this will make your skin sore.

Electric razors are quick to use, and you don't need water. But using foam, hot water and a disposable razor usually gives you a closer shave.

Electric razor

Disposable razor

Wet-shaving tips

Use a clean, sharp razor every time you shave. Follow these other handy tips for a painless experience:

* Look in a mirror to see what you're doing!
* Use foam or gel to lubricate your skin.
* Press the blade firmly to your face and pull it in the direction that the hair grows.
* Rinse out the blade in hot water after each stroke.
* Shave again in the opposite direction if you need to remove more hair.

After you've shaved, you should use a moisturizing cream or aftershave to soothe your skin. Be warned – some aftershaves can sting, especially if you've cut yourself.

Cuts and moles

It's very common to cut yourself when you start shaving, but it's not very painful. If you do get a cut, wash out any shaving cream, and press some cotton wool against it until the bleeding stops – this may take a few minutes.

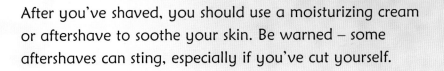

If you have hairs growing from any moles on your face, it's better to cut them off with fine scissors, as they can be sensitive to razors and might bleed.

How does it start?

Growing-up changes are caused by chemical messengers called hormones. There are many different hormones in your body, and they all do slightly different things. You might have already heard of a hormone called testosterone: it's one of the main chemicals that makes boys start to grow up.

Brain power

You can't make testosterone until your brain gives the right signal to your body. One night, when you're fast asleep, you will start to make a hormone called GnRH. This happens deep within your brain, in a part called the hypothalamus.

Once enough GnRH has been made, a bit in your brain called the pituitary gland is stimulated to produce two other hormones called LH and FSH. These travel through your body in the blood stream. In particular, they send a message to your testicles – the two balls that hang between your legs. Up until now, these haven't been doing much, except causing you pain when they get hit!

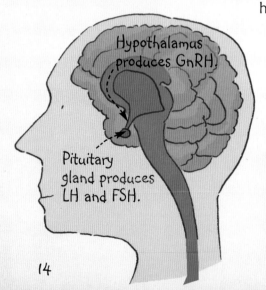

Hypothalamus produces GnRH.

Pituitary gland produces LH and FSH.

Testicle power

Once your testicles get the message from LH and FSH, they will start to make your sex hormones and sperm. Male sex hormones are called androgens; testosterone is one of these.

Androgens give instructions to other parts of your body. They tell your bones to grow, your voice to break, and so on. Androgens and other hormones can also affect your moods, making you feel low or irritable for no apparent reason.

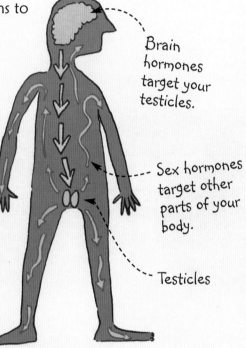

Brain hormones target your testicles.

Sex hormones target other parts of your body.

Testicles

For the rest of your life, androgens will be present in your blood. If your testicles got damaged, you could only make a small amount of androgens. The pain reminds you to protect these important bits!

Male or female?

Girls also make small amounts of testosterone, and boys make some female sex hormones too. It's the sudden build-up of these hormones that makes some boys' chests develop small breasts for a while. In a lot of ways, boys and girls aren't so very different.

What's it all about?

Puberty means your body is getting ready to make babies. You might have heard that storks deliver them to parents. You probably also know that some adults make up stories like this because they're embarrassed to talk about sex.

The messy truth

For a baby to start, a sperm from a man's body has to meet and join together with an ovum (egg) in a woman's body. This can happen when a woman and a man have sex. Here's how it works.

First, the man and woman get ready for sex, usually by kissing and cuddling each other – often called foreplay. This helps make the man's penis grow hard and stick up and away from his body. It may also make the woman's vagina release some slippery fluid. The vagina is a tube inside a woman's body with its opening between her legs. When it is wet, the man's hard penis can fit inside it.

Sperm

Then, the penis and the vagina can rub against each other. This makes a gooey fluid called semen squirt out of the man's penis. Semen contains millions of sperm. The sperm swim up inside the woman's body. If they find an egg there, one of the sperm might succeed in joining with it. And if this happens, a baby may start growing.

Just one sperm may join with an egg.

Sex and feelings

Couples don't have sex only to make babies. It can be a way of showing deep affection for each other, which is why it's also called "making love". Sex can make people feel good, but it can also make them feel bad if they do it with someone they don't really like or when they don't want to.

Uurrr! That's gross. I'm never doing that.

Me neither. Boys are yucky anyway.

Strange attraction

Sex might sound pretty disgusting to you. Or you might worry that you'll never meet anyone who wants to do it with you. Luckily, growing up makes you more sexually attractive. Your brain changes so that you find other people more attractive, too.

Sex without babies

When a couple has sex, there is always a chance that a baby can be made, even if the couple doesn't want this. So, when they want to have sex without making a baby, they can take precautions against it. This is called contraception. One type of contraception is a condom. This is a thin rubber cover which is put onto the man's penis before it goes into the woman's vagina. The semen gets caught in the end of the condom so the sperm can't swim up to the egg.

A condom

Down there ...

One place where you'll definitely notice some changes happening is between your legs. That's where your genitals are. They're also called sex organs, because you need them to have sex and make babies.

Take a closer look

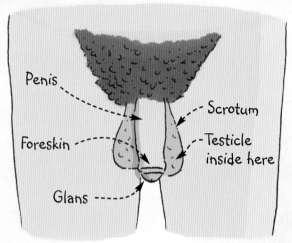

Penis

Foreskin

Glans

Scrotum

Testicle inside here

When you finish puberty, you will have all your pubic hair, your penis will have doubled in size, your testicles will be up to ten times bigger, and they'll be making lots of sperm.

The left testicle often hangs lower than the right one to stop them from banging together. They have to hang down because the inside of your body is too warm for your sperm. On cold days, your scrotum shrinks and pulls your testicles up nearer to your body to keep your sperm at the right temperature. Your penis shrinks when it gets cold, too.

The purplish, bell-shaped end of your penis is called the glans. It's very sensitive and so is all or partly covered by the foreskin – but not everybody has one (see page 22).

On the inside

Full-grown testicles make a mind-boggling 2,000 sperm every second. Behind each testicle is a long, coiled tube called an epididymis, which is where the sperm stay once they're made. Sperm can only live for a few days, which is why you keep making new ones all the time.

When they're ready to come out, sperm travel along the sperm ducts. At the same time, the seminal vesicles and prostate gland release fluids for the sperm to swim in, and to give them energy. The gloopy mixture of these fluids and sperm is called semen.

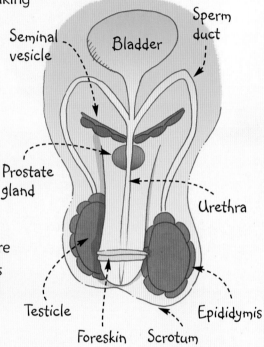

Seminal vesicle

Bladder

Sperm duct

Prostate gland

Urethra

Testicle

Foreskin

Scrotum

Epididymis

Going outside

Semen travels through the urethra and squirts out of the end of the penis. This is called an ejaculation. Only a teaspoonful of semen comes out in a few short spurts, but this is enough to contain millions of sperm. You won't be able to ejaculate until your body has started to make semen.

The urethra is also the tube that your urine (wee) comes out of when you go to the toilet. Don't worry – there is a valve at the back of your urethra that makes sure semen and urine don't come out at the same time.

... and up here

You're used to your penis hanging down. But sometimes it gets hard, and points up and away from your body. This is called an erection. You need to have an erection to ejaculate semen.

Some boys get erections from an early age. Most boys find they get them every day when they're going through puberty.

How does it happen?

Blood is always pumping in and out of your penis, but a valve can make more blood flow in than normal, and less flow out. The extra blood fills up a spongy substance called erectile tissue, making your penis bigger and harder. You can feel it as soon as it starts to swell. After a while, the valve lets the blood flow out again, and your erection goes down.

You'll probably get an erection if you think about sex, or if you see someone you fancy. Often, though, you can get an erection without knowing why, and when you really don't want one. This is just your body and brain getting used to your new hormones.

Make it go away!

Erections can be embarrassing, because there are times when you're sure that everyone can tell you've got one. They can be less obvious if you wear briefs rather than boxer shorts, or if you wear baggy trousers. Most erections will go away after a few minutes, and if you try to concentrate on something else it can help to get rid of them. This is much easier said than done, of course.

Bodily fluids

The first time your penis squirts out semen, it can be very surprising, but it's a nice feeling. Some boys wake up to find it has happened while they were asleep, during a "wet dream". These are pleasant dreams that are often, but not always, about sex. Semen is wet, and it leaves a mark on your pyjamas or sheets, but it washes out easily. Some boys have a lot of wet dreams, but not everybody has them.

Once their bodies have started producing semen, boys can make themselves ejaculate by rubbing their penis up and down. This is called masturbation. It's a natural thing to do, and some boys do it every day because it feels good. You don't have to masturbate, though, and some boys never do. The feeling you get when semen squirts out is called an orgasm (also called "coming"), and it happens when the muscles in your penis contract. Sometimes this makes the semen squirt out quite far; other times it just oozes out.

Other boys look different

When you're in the changing room or the school showers, you'll probably notice other boys' penises. Don't worry, everybody glances at other people sometimes. You'll soon notice that penises can look different in some ways.

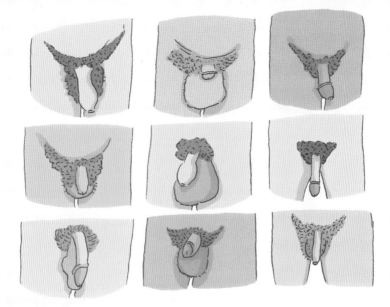

Jackets not required

When they are born, all boys have a foreskin covering all or part of their glans. But in some countries and religions, boys have their foreskin removed – usually a few days after birth. The operation to do this is called circumcision. Whether you do or don't have a foreskin, your penis will work in the same way as everybody else's.

Boys who haven't been circumcised will find that their foreskin gets pulled back a bit when they have an erection, exposing the glans. If you have a tight foreskin, this won't happen at first, but it should loosen as you get older.

Make it bigger

Nearly all boys, especially teenagers, worry about the size of their penis. When they're floppy, penises change in size all the time, and they can get really small when it's cold. But erect penises don't vary in size as much as floppy ones do. Big ones also get hard and stick out when erect, but they don't necessarily get much longer or thicker.

There's nothing you can do to make your penis longer. Although boys tease each other about it, you'll find out that girls generally don't care.

Bends

You might have a slight bend to your penis, which you'll probably only notice when it's erect. It might bend up, or to the left or right. Some boys have a really obvious bend, while other boys' penises look straight. Both kinds are normal. You won't give yourself a bend, and you can't make one go away.

Bumps and moles

If you look closely, you might see moles or little bumps in various places on your penis and scrotum. These are very common and are nothing to worry about. You only need to tell a doctor if they start to change, for example if they get bigger or become itchy.

Your feelings

Growing up can make you feel moody sometimes. You'll have to deal with a changing body, lots of hormones, new emotions and also your first responsibilities as a young adult. It can help to know that almost everybody finds this time of life difficult, however much they try to hide it.

Friends

Making friends isn't always easy. People can be shy, even if they don't act it, and it can take time to meet people you get on with. If you're kind to others, they'll usually be kind to you. Lots of people like to be part of a group, and having friends can make your life happier. At times, it can seem as if it's more important than anything else to fit in, but you should never be pressurized into doing something that you don't want to do.

Parents

It's not unusual to argue with your parents as you get older. They may forget how much you've grown up, and they can find it hard to let you make your own decisions.

When your parents make rules, it's often because they want to protect you, not because they don't respect you. Even though it can be frustrating, you will have to compromise between getting your own way and earning your parents' trust.

Fancying people

As you get older, it's natural to start feeling sexually attracted to other people. You might imagine touching or kissing them, or just being near to them. This is called fantasizing, and it's something many boys and girls do, especially when they masturbate. Fantasizing about someone is a safe and natural way of exploring your emotions. And don't worry if your fantasies seem odd.

At this stage, people often want to start dating and kissing. Don't let anyone pressurize you into this before you're ready, even if everybody else seems to be doing it.

Many boys wonder whether they are gay – which means they are sexually attracted to other boys. It can be confusing because it's quite common to fancy someone the same sex as you, especially when you're growing up. And it's perfectly possible to fancy both girls and boys. It's something you need to work out for yourself as you grow up. Lots of boys tease each other about it, but there's nothing wrong with being gay. It is much more acceptable to date people of the same sex than it used to be.

Power and responsibility

By the time you finish puberty, you will be able to do things that you couldn't do before. Growing up gives you new powers, and each one brings with it great responsibility.

Pregnancy

A growing baby is called a fetus.

When a baby is made during sex, the woman becomes pregnant. This means that the baby is growing inside her; it stays there for nine months before being born. A man can't get pregnant, but as soon as he starts making sperm, he can make a woman pregnant if he has sex with her. When a baby is made, it's his responsibility as well as hers.

Many people feel ready to have sex when they're still young, but it takes a long time before they are ready to look after a baby.

Stronger, taller, faster

As your body grows, you will gain more power. You will be able to run faster, lift heavier weights, and punch harder than you ever could before. This is very exciting, but it can be dangerous. For example, if you like play-fighting and wrestling, you'll have to be more careful not to damage the people and objects around you.

I am Teenage Boy! Marvel at my feats of wonder!

I want to be like you

Role models can be an important part of growing up. You might look up to an older brother, a friend at school, or a famous person. But you might not turn out the same as them. Everyone ends up looking different, and being good at different things.

Don't force yourself to be like someone you're not, and don't be surprised if you start to become interested in different things from your friends.

Mind matters

Most of the growing-up changes described in this book are about your body. But don't forget that your mind will change as well, although not as much.

Your brain will have to learn to get used to your new body, for example when you're playing sports or singing. In particular, your brain will be affected by your hormones, which can make it hard to concentrate sometimes. You might also spend more time thinking about grown-up things, like sex. It's important that you don't get so caught up in your daydreams and emotions that you stop paying attention to your family, your friends and your schoolwork.

Good food

Believe it or not, you really will deal with the ups and downs of growing up better if you're eating a good diet. Food is the fuel your body uses to help you grow, and without the right kinds of food, it's much harder to stay healthy. A balanced diet gives you energy and equips you better to fight illness.

Food groups

You have to eat lots of different foods to get all the nutrients (goodness) you need. Dieticians divide food into five groups.

1. **Bread, potatoes, rice, pasta and cereals**
   These are starchy carbohydrates and you should eat lots, for energy.

2. **Fruit and vegetables (fresh, frozen or canned)**
   Eat at least five portions a day. These give you essential vitamins and minerals, as well as fibre, which helps protect you from diseases. (Potatoes aren't included in this group, but beans and lentils are.)

3. **Meat, fish, eggs, nuts, beans, lentils**
   Eat moderate amounts of these foods. They provide protein, which helps you to grow.

4. **Milk, cheese, yogurt**
   Eat moderate amounts. These foods contain calcium, which helps you to develop strong bones and teeth.

5. **Foods containing fat and/or sugar**
   Don't eat too many of these. Examples of foods that are mostly fat and sugar include milk shakes, ice cream and biscuits.

How much?

During puberty, you need as much food or even more than an adult man because you're growing so fast. Hunger is the best guide to how much to eat, not your appearance. Eat when you're hungry but don't keep eating once you're full. You are going to put on weight just because your body is getting taller and more muscular, even if you don't get fatter.

This chart shows what proportion of your food should come from each group. You should eat most from groups 1 and 2 and least from group 5.

More about eating

Breakfast

Don't skip breakfast. Your body uses energy even while you're asleep and you need to replace it in the morning. A healthy breakfast stops you feeling weak and sluggish, improves your concentration and makes you function better all round.

Food and teeth

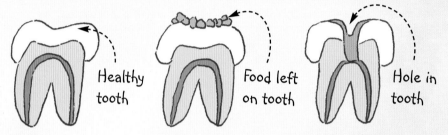

Healthy tooth

Food left on tooth

Hole in tooth

You will have your adult teeth by the time you're about 13, and they have to last you for life. If food specks are left on them, your teeth will eventually develop holes called cavities.

You need to brush thoroughly twice a day, especially before you go to bed. Brush up and down to dislodge food from between the teeth, and learn how to floss. Change your toothbrush at least every three months, and try to visit a dentist twice a year. Remember, all sugary foods and drinks are bad for your teeth.

Angle your brush to clean the backs of your teeth.

Ready meals versus fresh

The food in most ready meals has been altered in some way in a factory. In this processing, nutrients may have been lost and chemicals such as artificial colourings and flavourings may have been added. Some researchers think these can cause ill health, and dieticians generally recommend eating food which is as fresh and unprocessed as possible.

Junk food

Junk food has little or no goodness in it. Usually it contains a lot of sugar, fat or salt, and is often fattening too. Examples of junk food are sugary drinks, sweets, lollies, bought biscuits and cakes, and salted snacks like crisps. It's hard to avoid junk foods completely, but try to choose healthy snacks such as fruit whenever you can.

Meals or snacks?

Some people like to eat three meals in a day, while others prefer to snack on smaller amounts of food throughout the day. It can be healthy to eat many small snacks, but you're more likely to get a balanced diet by eating regular meals. And remember that meals are a social event as well as an excuse to eat. You need to consider that you'll be missing out, and might even upset your family and friends, if you decide to snack a lot and not eat meals.

Keep on moving

Your body is designed to be used – so don't be shy of walking, jumping, dancing or playing sports. Regular exercise makes you feel more alert, and less stressed. It also helps you to sleep better. Best of all, exercise helps to prevent many illnesses, from heart disease to depression.

How much?

To get fit and stay fit, you really need to exercise for at least half an hour every day (preferably an hour). This sounds a lot, but it can include walking to school, so long as you walk fast. Walking up stairs is also a good way to get exercise without having to try too hard. However, at least twice a week, your exercise needs to be fairly strenuous – it needs to get your heart beating fast.

Not *too* much

Boys grow muscle at different rates, and some boys are just naturally more muscley than others. Lifting weights will make your muscles bigger – as long as you're eating the right food as well. But it can be dangerous to do too much strength training before you are fully grown. It's frustrating if you're a late starter, but do be careful.

But I hate sports

Playing a sport is a great way to keep fit, but there are plenty of other ways to exercise if you don't like sport or competing, or if you just aren't very co-ordinated. Even if you do play a lot of sport, it's important to vary the kind of exercise you get. You need to build up your stamina (the ability to keep going for a long time), as well as your strength, and your suppleness (the ability to bend and stretch your body). Here are a few suggestions:

Swimming

Fast walking

Tennis

Football

Martial arts

Cycling

Energetic dancing

Rest and sleep

Growing up is hard work for your body and mind, so you need time to rest and recover. In sleep, your body repairs itself and your dreams may help you to learn and make sense of things that have happened to you. Most 8-10-year-olds need about 10 hours sleep a night, 11-15s about 9.

Filthy beasts

As you grow up, you'll start to sweat more. Adult sweat can be thick and smelly, and it often appears when you're nervous – not just when you're exercising. Keeping clean is good for you and makes you more pleasant to be with.

Sweating and smelling

The best way to get rid of sweat and smells is to wash every day. After you wash, you can put on deodorants – which kill the bacteria that make the smells; or you can use antiperspirants – which cut down on how much you sweat. Most things labelled as deodorants also contain antiperspirants.

By the time you've grown hair in your armpits, you'll probably need to use a deodorant under your arms every morning. Just remember that deodorants aren't a substitute for washing!

Roll-on or spray?

Most deodorants can be applied using either a roll-on stick, or an aerosol spray can. Both work equally well at stopping smells, but aerosols can be bad for people with asthma or allergies, and some of the gases they contain harm the environment.

Getting smeggy

If you have a foreskin, you'll find that you can roll it back further as you get older. Once it is loose enough for you to expose the whole glans, you will see that you have started making smegma. This is a natural and healthy lubricant that all boys' penises make every day – even if they're circumcised. If you have a foreskin, the smegma may build up underneath it into little white flakes, which smell bad. You need to wash these flakes away every day or two. To do this, gently roll back your foreskin and wash the glans with warm water. You can use a mild soap if you want, but don't use gels as the skin here is very sensitive.

Hygiene and health

Washing isn't just about getting rid of bad smells. Bacteria live on your skin, and if you let them grow and reproduce, you're more likely to get an infection. Bacteria like to live in warm, dark and hairy places, so be sure to wash your armpits, bum, genitals and your hair regularly.

Bacteria live in your clothes as well as on your skin. Even if you've had a shower, putting on dirty or sweaty clothes will make you smell, and isn't healthy. It's a particularly good idea to change your underwear every day.

From the neck up

Almost everyone gets spots on their face when they're a teenager. You can also get them on your back, or other parts of your body. Trying to get rid of them or hide them can be a nightmare, but at least you're not alone.

Too oily

Everyone's skin produces a kind of oil called sebum. Without it, your skin and hair would dry out. But the changes in your hormone levels, especially testosterone, can send sebum production out of control. Result: spots and greasy hair. Many people's hair gets so greasy that they have to wash it every day.

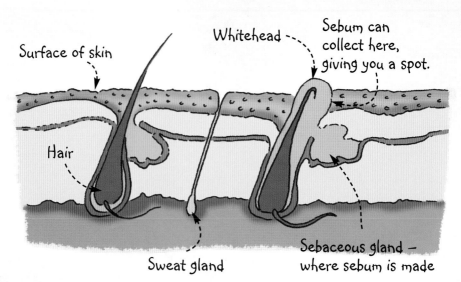

Surface of skin

Whitehead

Sebum can collect here, giving you a spot.

Hair

Sweat gland

Sebaceous gland – where sebum is made

Dealing with spots

Different people swear by different spot remedies. The best thing is to find out which works well for you.

Wash your face twice a day with mild, unperfumed or antiseptic soap. Use warm water and your bare hands.

Keep your hands and nails clean and don't play with your spots.

Try one of the spot treatments you can buy from the chemist's.

If your spots are really bad, don't put up with them – ask your pharmacist or doctor what to do.

Eat a healthy diet. Many people believe that certain foods give them spots, although experts haven't found any convincing evidence for this.

It's hard not to worry about how you look, but try to remember that other people are more interested in you than your face.

Squeezing

Some doctors say you should never squeeze your spots, but here are a few precautions to take if you do:

* Wash your hands first.
* Use your fingers, not your nails.
* Only squeeze blackheads or whiteheads, nothing red or angry.
* Stop if nothing happens, or if clear fluid or blood comes out.
* Dab on an antiseptic, such as tea tree oil, afterwards.
* Wash your hands again.

It's different for girls

You might not be very interested in girls at the moment, but the chances are that you will be one day. Girls come in all different shapes and sizes, just as boys do.

What do they get?

Girls go through a long list of growing-up changes. Some of them are very similar to the changes boys go through.

They get taller and heavier.

Their breasts start to develop.

Their hips get wider.

Their faces get longer.

Their voices get a bit deeper.

They grow pubic hair and armpit hair.

They start to sweat more.

Their skin and hair may get greasier.

Their sex organs develop.

They start to have periods.

Hormones at work

Girls start puberty in exactly the same way as boys –
when the right hormones are released in their brains. But
girls don't have testicles. Instead, they have ovaries.
Ovaries hold a girl's eggs, and make a girl's sex hormones.
These give instructions to change her body into a
woman's, just as androgens change boys into men.

On average, girls start puberty a few months before boys.
For a while, girls might be taller than boys their age, but
they tend to finish growing earlier than boys do. The
changes that happen to girls get them ready to have
babies, and also make them sexually attractive – just like
the changes that happen to boys.

What do girls look
like with no
clothes on?

Girls on the inside ...

Some of the most important changes that happen to a girl take place deep inside her body. That's because most of her sex organs are safely hidden away inside her, and that's where babies are made.

A girl's sex organs are low down in her tummy.

What's in there?

A girl has two ovaries, two fallopian tubes, a womb (sometimes called a uterus), and a vagina. These will all get bigger, along with the rest of her body.

Fallopian tubes

Ovary

Ovary

A girl has all her eggs stored in her ovaries when she is born, but they only become active after she starts puberty.

The vagina leads to the outside of a girl's body, with its opening between her legs.

Womb

Cervix – a passageway between the womb and vagina

Vagina

40

Monthly cycle

Roughly once a month, one egg from one ovary is released into the nearest fallopian tube. Meanwhile, the girl's womb has been building up a thick, soft lining. If the egg joins with a sperm in the tube, it can then attach itself to the lining in the womb and grow into a baby.

When an egg doesn't join with a sperm within a few days, it breaks up. Then the womb lining, which is mostly made of blood, is shed slowly through the girl's vagina. This is called having a period. Unless a girl is pregnant, it happens to her every four weeks or so.

Coping with periods

Period bleeding can take up to seven days, even though only two to four tablespoons of blood come out. To stop blood getting on her clothes, a girl can use a tampon – which fits inside her vagina, or a sanitary towel – which sticks to the inside of her knickers. She has to change the tampon or towel every few hours.

Tampon

Sanitary towel

Having periods is a totally normal and healthy process, but it can be painful for a day or two. Girls simply carry on with their everyday lives. Before a period starts, the hormones that control it can make a girl feel low and a bit unwell. This is called PMS, or "pre-menstrual syndrome". Not all girls get this, though.

... and on the outside

Girls' external sex organs aren't very obvious. But, just like boys' genitals, they grow during puberty, and they're very sensitive. Their proper name is the vulva.

The vulva

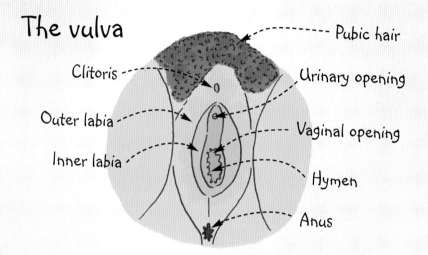

Clitoris

Outer labia

Inner labia

Pubic hair

Urinary opening

Vaginal opening

Hymen

Anus

The vulva is cushioned by two thick folds of skin called the outer labia (or lips). These will grow hair during puberty. Inside are two smaller folds called the inner labia.

At the front, where the inner labia meet, is a small pea-shaped bump called the clitoris. Everyone starts off with a bump here, but when a boy is growing in his mother's womb, this becomes his penis. Just like a penis, a girl's clitoris is very sensitive to touch.

The vaginal opening is stretchy: tampons will fit through it; so will a man's penis during sex; and a baby comes through it to be born. The vaginal opening may be covered by a thin layer of skin called the hymen. Often this wears away while the girl is still young, especially if she does a lot of sport. It will wear away completely as she gets older.

Nearby parts

The tiny hole where a girl's urine comes out, called the urinary opening, is a bit further back than the clitoris. It isn't really part of her vulva because it has nothing to do with sex.

Her anus (where solid waste comes out when she goes to the toilet) isn't part of the vulva either, but it's very close.

Breasts and bras

Often the first growing-up change that boys notice about girls is their breasts. These have various functions: they make milk for a baby soon after it is born (milk comes out through the nipples); they look attractive; and they're sensitive to touch.

Breasts move about as a girl walks, and can be quite heavy. To help support them, most girls wear a bra. These come in many shapes and sizes, to match different types of breast, and different outfits. Bra sizes are measured in numbers and letters. The number is the measurement around the girl's ribcage; the letters tell you how big each bra cup is.

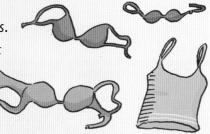

A girl's life

Girls worry about the changes that are happening to them just as much as boys do. They even have a lot of the same problems.

Shaving

Girls don't need to shave their faces, but just like boys they grow hair in other places. Many girls shave under their arms, and also their legs – which are much easier to cut than your face. Some girls also trim their pubic hair, so that it doesn't poke out of their swimsuits. Instead of shaving, girls sometimes use creams or wax to remove hair.

Sticky stuff

As they get older, girls find that they release a small amount of fluid from their vagina. This fluid is cleansing and moisturizing, and it's perfectly healthy, although it can be a bit off-putting until they get used to it.

Girls don't ejaculate semen, but they can have sexy dreams like boys do; they just don't wake up as wet as boys. Girls can masturbate, too – usually by stroking their clitoris – which increases the amount of fluid in their vagina, and can give them an orgasm.

Body image

Girls can feel under pressure to look like glamorous celebrities, often before they've finished growing. They might worry that they are too fat, or that their breasts are too big or too small. Some people think that this anxiety can even lead to depression and eating disorders. Boys worry about their looks as well, but usually less.

At school and at home

It can seem as if girls find it much easier to make friends than boys do, and get along better with adults. It's true they tend to grow up earlier than boys, mentally as well as physically, but this doesn't mean their life is any easier. Girls can be shy, too, especially around boys. And girls bully each other just as much as boys do, whether it's by being mean to someone, or not talking to them, or even by beating them up.

Parents can be stricter with their daughters, perhaps because they're worried about them getting hurt, or even pregnant. This means they might not be allowed out as often, or as late, as boys are.

45

Trials of life

As you get older, you'll find yourself in difficult situations.
Here are some of the issues you might have to deal with.

Drugs

Dangerous drugs include alcohol and nicotine (in cigarettes),
as well as drugs that are illegal (against the law) like
cannabis, cocaine, ecstasy, LSD, and heroin. These drugs can
damage your body and mind. Don't ever try a drug just
because someone else wants you to; remember that different
people can have different reactions to the same drugs. And
some drugs, including glue, lighter gas and aerosols, can kill
the very first time someone uses them. It's easy to become
dependent on drugs, and hard to give them up. This can ruin
your relationships and job prospects as well as your health.

* Most heavy
smokers die
from smoking.

* Cannabis-
users often suffer
from depression.

* Binge drinking
can damage your
developing brain.

Bullying

If you're being bullied, don't suffer alone. Talk about it with
an adult you trust. They may be able to help you decide
what to do, or even help you find a way to stop the
bullying. And remember, it's not your fault – no one
deserves to be bullied.

Safe sex

Safe sex doesn't just mean using contraception to avoid pregnancy. If someone has an infection in their sex organs, they can pass it on during sex. Many sexually transmitted infections (STIs) can be cured if they're treated early, but some can be very serious, even life-threatening. For example, HIV is a virus that can give people a disease called AIDS, and there is no cure for this. It damages your blood, and makes it hard for you to fight off everyday infections. People can pass HIV on to each other if they have sex. Using a condom correctly gives protection against most STIs, including HIV.

The right to say no

Sometimes, people try to persuade or even force children to do things they are too young to do, or that are illegal. This could include taking drugs, or having sexual contact with them. If anyone touches you in a sexual way, or puts pressure on you to do something that makes you feel uncomfortable, tell them to stop. Whether it's someone your own age, an adult relative or a complete stranger, no-one has the right to do this to you, and you always have the right to say no. You should also tell an adult you trust what has happened.

Adults who are sexually attracted to children are called paedophiles. They can be very sly, and may use the internet to pretend to be young in the hope of persuading children to meet them. Be careful who you make friends with.

Index

First published in 2006 by Usborne Publishing Ltd, Usborne House, 83-85 Saffron Hill, London EC1N 8RT,
England. www.usborne.com Copyright © 2006 Usborne Publishing Ltd. The name Usborne and the
devices ⊕ ♀ are Trade Marks of Usborne Publishing Ltd. All rights reserved. No part of this publication
may be reproduced, stored in a retrieval system or transmitted in any form or by any means, electronic,
mechanical, photocopying, recording or otherwise, without the prior permission of the publisher.
Printed in China.